1942

A YEAR TO REMEMBER

DRINK MORE M
OR Y

1942

A YEAR TO REMEMBER

by

Richard Hease

in association with
British Pathe News
and
Dennis Fairey and Associates

A Year to Remember -1942

First published in book form in Great Britain by Mistral Publishing Ltd. 1991 in association with British Pathe News Ltd.

ISBN - 1 874053 05 7

A CIP catalogue record for this book is available from the British Library.

Printed and bound by Waterside Press, Hatfield, England.

Design and Typesetting by Dennis Fairey & Associates Ltd., Chiltern House, 184 High Street, Berkhamsted, Herts HP4 3AP

1942

NEWS

Pathe Review

We are all part of history, wherever we are and whatever we are doing. World events shape our memories and for most of the 20th Century those events were filmed and explained by Pathe. Pathe News captured history in motion, creating a living chronicle of a turbulent century.

The following pages contain actual pictures taken from the Pathe newsreels accompanied by the slightly edited version of the original transcripts which became a very distinctive style over the years.

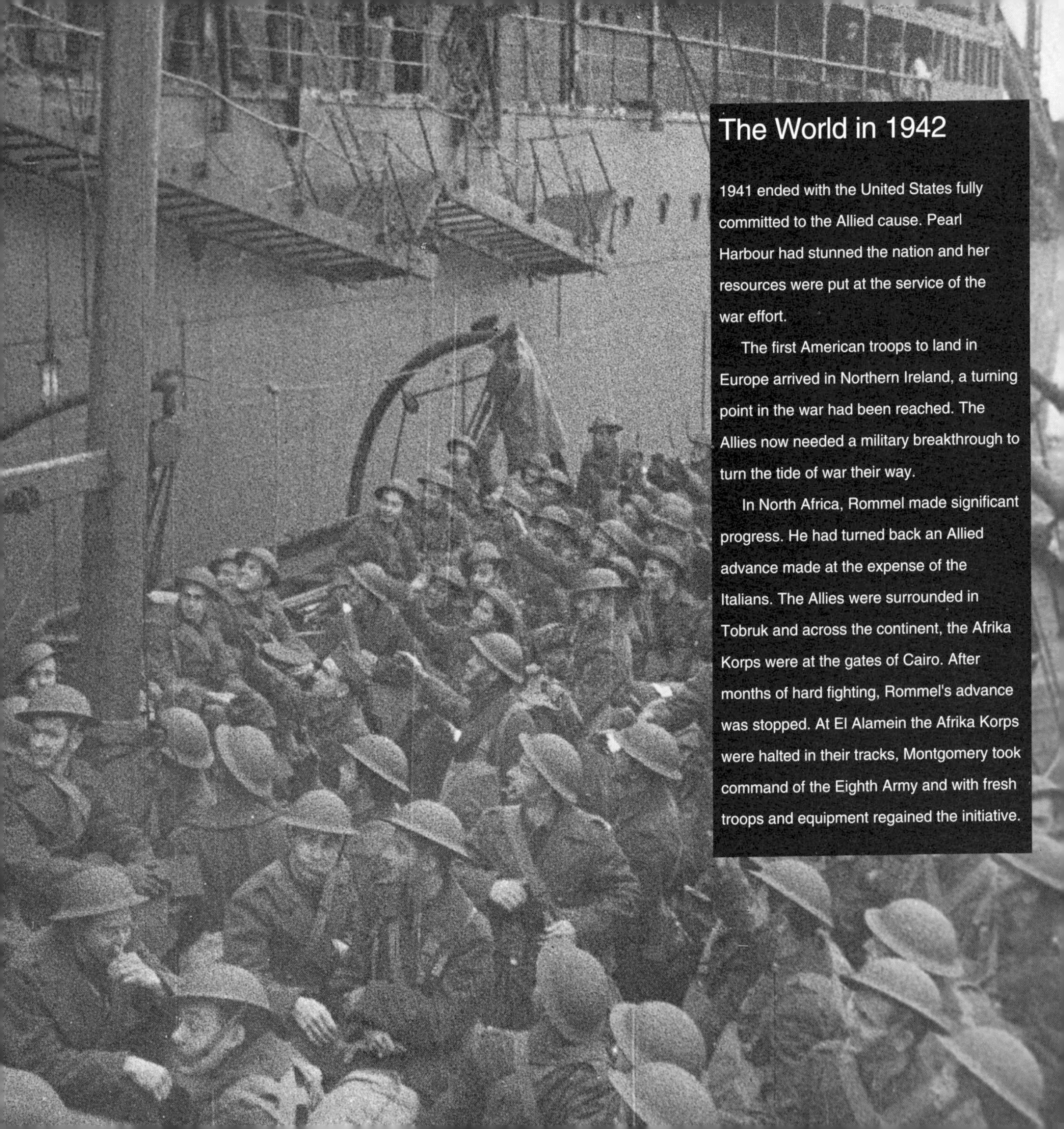

The World in 1942

1941 ended with the United States fully committed to the Allied cause. Pearl Harbour had stunned the nation and her resources were put at the service of the war effort.

The first American troops to land in Europe arrived in Northern Ireland, a turning point in the war had been reached. The Allies now needed a military breakthrough to turn the tide of war their way.

In North Africa, Rommel made significant progress. He had turned back an Allied advance made at the expense of the Italians. The Allies were surrounded in Tobruk and across the continent, the Afrika Korps were at the gates of Cairo. After months of hard fighting, Rommel's advance was stopped. At El Alamein the Afrika Korps were halted in their tracks, Montgomery took command of the Eighth Army and with fresh troops and equipment regained the initiative.

Churchill on Victory in desert "End of the Beginning" speech at the Mansion House.

It was a significant victory, prompting Churchill to make one of his most famous speeches...

" This is not the end. It is not even the beginning of the end. But it is perhaps the end of the beginning."

In Asia, Japan made steady progress, Malaya, Singapore and the Solomon Islands fell. Burmah was under pressure. The Americans put their considerable navy into action against the Japanese. The battle of the Coral Sea made full use of naval air power and the Japanese met defeat at the world's biggest naval engagement so far, the Battle of Midway, giving Allied morale another boost.

By December the British were starting to push the Japanese back in Burmah.

In Europe Hitler's troops fought the vicious battle of Stalingrad - urban warfare at its most horrific. The Eastern front was draining men and equipment for little gain. The RAF started its policy of saturation bombing to weaken the morale of the German nation and many heroic figures emerged.

By 1941 the Germans had formulated their plans to rid Europe of its 11 million Jews; the Final Solution was worked out by Reinhard Heydrich and his colleagues. By June it was estimated that one million Jews had been killed. Orders to clear the Jewish ghetto in Warsaw claimed 50,000 more lives.

A powerful oration from Hitler.

First American troops to arrive in Northern Ireland.

S
A
ALL
REGULA
SAVING
ROAD

Crowd hears
Lord Beaverbrook's call
to open a second front
against Germany.

NEWS FROM SINGAPORE

January

"Planes! We must have more planes" was the cry that came from Malaya and was heard above the din of battle in Norway, France, Crete and Britain. Early in December, just prior to the first Japanese raid, a consignment of Beaufort aircraft arrived at Singapore, fresh from Commonwealth factories for impending action.

Some of the last evacuees from Singapore arrive in Britain.

North of Singapore on the Malay Peninsular, Australian troops helped make every inch of the way to the Fortress Island a death trap for the yellow plague infecting the Straits Settlement. In a jungle waterway a gunboat patrolled on the look-out for Japs, with the possibility of coming across hundreds of them scurrying about the undergrowth and scaling trees like monkeys.

The first picture of Singapore's taste of aerial war revealed the damage done to Raffles Square, in the heart of the Island's shopping centre. Department stores, shops and business houses, it was the same old story, with street clocks registering the early hours of morning when death and destruction came at the hands of Hitler's yellow brothers.

Nurses and Civil Defence workers worked tirelessly throughout the day tending the wounded and scouring the wreckage for tragic evidence of the horrors of the night. It was all very typical of the Nazi-Nipponese brotherhood.

Temporarily stunned by the Japanese blitz, the people of Singapore bought their morning papers in the rubble-strewn city streets, and learned that war had come to the Pacific. An ironical revelation after a night of horrible slaughter.

Beach Road Police Station became a busy place as Japanese nationals were rounded-up for internment. British and Malay policemen collected them for transportation to secret camps. Since that first treacherous blow the island rapidly accommodated itself to a virtual state of siege. This part of the Empire called out for strong and immediate action.

Argyll and Sutherland Highlanders prepare to defend Singapore.

Churchill in Ottowa.

CHURCHILL IN THE U. S. A.

The Prime Minister's oration in the Senate Chamber was acclaimed in both countries as an historic masterpiece.

"Members of the Senate and of the House of Representatives of the U.S. I feel greatly honoured that you should have invited me to enter the United States Senate Chamber and address the representatives of both branches of Congress . The fact that my American forebears have for so many generations played their part in the life of the United States and that here I am, an Englishman, welcomed in your midst makes this experience one of the most moving and thrilling in my life, which is already long and has not been entirely uneventful. I wish indeed that my mother, whose memory I cherish across the vale of years, could have been here to have seen me. By the way, I cannot help to reflect it, that if my father had been American and my mother British, instead of the other way round, I might have got here on my own" said Churchill.

"I'm so glad to be able to place before you members of the Senate and of the House of Representatives, at this moment when you are entering the war, the proof that with proper weapons and proper organisation we are able to beat the life out of the savage Nazi. Lastly if you will forgive me for saying it, to me the best tidings of all, the United States, united as never before, has drawn the sword for freedom and cast away the scabbard".

Churchill piloting seaplane from U.S. to Bermuda.

Not long after the enlistment queue, American troops march on parade.

NORMANDIE FIRE

February

During the Conversion of the 'Normandie' (recently named Lafayette) into a troop carrier, a fire broke out in the 83,000-ton liner. Investigations established, apparently beyond all doubt, that the sparks which started the fire came from an acetylene blow-lamp which was being used close to bales of inflammable material. Orders were given to move the bales but they were shifted only two or three feet away. Although all suggestions of sabotage were officially discounted the whole business appeared rather suspicious.

Thousands of workers had to flee for their lives as flames roared through the one-time French luxury liner. The dockside at New York harbour was eventually cleared as firemen and apparatus from all over Manhattan fought the stubborn blaze that raged for four hours. Ambulance men were kept busy as many casualties were taken away from the fire-swept ship.

While the fire was confined to the three top decks a new danger presented itself. The closure of the fire proof doors prevented the escape of hundreds of tons of water poured into her by the fire hoses. Gradually the ship became top-heavy and took on a dangerous list which was ultimately responsible for her capsizing. Early in the morning she toppled over and lay in the soft mud in the docks. Not sabotage? - many wondered.

Firefighting boats tackling the blaze on the 'Normandie'.

ON LEAVE IN CAIRO

March

The converted River Nile boat 'Arabia' was a dream ship come true for troops serving in the Western desert. Nobby and Ginger (so they were called), were given seven days leave in Cairo and since hearing a great deal about the houseboat, decided to board the 'Arabia' to sample its pleasures.

The leave ship was the original idea of two officers who (realising a need for a home from home) set the scheme going and even installed a sergeant as receptionist. It was paradise after the sweat, blood and tears of the desert, and even a waiter was present to bring tea while a fellow relaxed in an easy chair. Nobby and Ginger felt like a couple of millionaires, enjoying home comforts, at a cost well within their means.

They both spent the night in a Cabin de Luxe and an early morning cup of tea the next day helped to bring them back to earth. Breakfast was followed by a nice hot bath and those desert meals of 'sand and bully' seemed like an ugly dream.

Nobby and Ginger arrive for a well earned break aboard the 'Arabia'.

With six whole days ahead of them, Nobby and Ginger decided to see the sights of Cairo, two light-hearted soldiers wondering where to visit first. Nobby was a bit of a camera fiend with an eye for the picturesque and Ginger kept a sharp lookout for a little souvenir which more likely than not was made in Birmingham. Walking through the 'Mouski', the oldest bazaar quarter in Cairo, was a grand adventure, followed by a ride round the Pyramids on a couple of cruiser model camels.

To round off the day there was dancing on board 'Arabia' and girls in the womens' services would come to the houseboat for a tea dance. Music on the Nile and the soft lapping of water against the boat brought luxury and romance to the desert.

A chance to relax and watch the world go by.

Camera at the ready, the boys take a look around Cairo.

ANGLO-RUSSIAN TREATY

May

Early one morning in May a powerful four-engined Soviet bomber came in to land at a Northern aerodrome, with few people knowing of its arrival. Out of it stepped the Soviet peoples' Commissar for Foreign Affairs, Mr Molotov, clad in a heavy fur-lined flying kit. He had just flown from the U.S.S.R. with close secrecy surrounding his arrival.

Nearby a Guard of Honour presented arms in salute to the important diplomat. It was the start of what was to prove an epoch-making visit. The crew of the aircraft, which included a famous Soviet airman were soon at home with their comrades in the RAF.

At the local station a special train was waiting to take Mr Molotov to London. As it drew out, he settled down to an English breakfast to enjoy the scenery with the high officials who travelled with him. Mr Molotov's presence was one of the best-kept secrets of the war. At a station outside London, Mr Eden was there to welcome his Russian collaborator and with Mr Maisky (who had joined the train earlier), left for a meeting with Mr Churchill at Number 10 Downing Street.

Long before the story was to be made public, these pictures were taken to represent the historic events leading to the great Anglo-Soviet treaty, the conclusion of a 20-year treaty of alliance with full partnership in war and peace.

"...We shall work together for victory over our common enemy..."

That victory was brought nearer by this wise and far seeing instrument of mutual assistance. At the Foreign Office the grand alliance was documented as signatures were appended to the document by the representatives of the high contracting parties. A full understanding was also reached with a regard to creating this year a second front in Europe this year.

Once again the great aircraft set forth, this time carrying Mr Molotov to the United States, whose willing participation in the great alliance completed the invincible trilogy of nations. The new treaty had an electrifying effect all over the world. It was the power switch that set in motion the machinery to grind the last vestige of tyranny out of Europe.

Churchill meets Molotov and Maisky to sign Anglo-Russian treaty.

GOERING IN ITALY

June

In Italy, Pathe's cameras were present at the arrival of Hitler's number one man and the news story of that day reflects Pathe's distinctive style, combined with the feelings of animosity of the period.

"Lucky, lucky, lucky here comes the Director of Economy, Chief of Defence, Prime Minister of Prussia, Air Minister and Hitler's number one man, Field Marshal Goering. The Nazi 'Thin Man' has come to see his Luftwaffe pilots in Italy and as his wife has sent all his medals to the cleaners, old skin and bone has a look round to see what he can pick-up cheaply. And now standing on a soap box filled with reinforced concrete, the Reichmarshal speaks to a number of Nazis picking the bones out of Italy after a spell on the African front. With the grace of a baby hippopotamus, the Field Marshal moves to an anti-aircraft gun site hoping to heaven it's working properly. Well, so long tiny, we'll be round your way soon."

Field Marshal Goering inspects Luftwaffe crews in Italy.

NEWS BRIEFS

July

General Eisenhower, the newly-appointed American C-in-C in Europe, took office in London to establish a European theatre of operations for the United States Forces.

The Texan General at 51 is clear-thinking, resolute and tough. At one time he was General MacArthur's right-hand man. General Eisenhower kept a close contact with our Chief of Combined Operations, Lord Louis Mountbatten. The combination was a strong one and worked well for the Allied cause.

Four American airmen who took part in the Independence Day raid on the Netherlands were decorated at an American bomber station in Britain. Their aircraft had been so heavily hit by flak that it came down and hit the ground. But they flew on, shot up a gun emplacement on the way and made home on one engine.

General Eisenhower planning strategy for his new role as C-in-C Europe.

SINKING OF U.S. AIRCRAFT CARRIER LEXINGTON

July

This report presented a further pictorial on the sinking of the 'U.S. Lexington' in the great battle of the Coral Sea.

A dramatic movie camera record revealed for the first time the death struggle of the 33,000-ton aircraft carrier.

After successfully weathering attack after attack by Jap dive bombers, internal explosions finally sealed her doom; with smoke and flames spouting from the carrier. More than 2,000 of her crew abandoned ship. This was the end of a great ship, yet her loss was avenged four times over a few weeks later.

Among survivors of the Lexington were the seven Patten brothers, seen here being greeted by their father who is on Navy recruiting duty. A great homecoming for the U.S. Navy's most famous family team.

Thousands of their town folk in Portland, Oregon turned out to give them a real home-town welcome. The Pattens were a family of fighters.

Aircraft on deck of Lexington.

U.S. pilots on Lexington scramble for the battle of the Coral Sea.

The seven Patten brothers.

JAPS RAID PORT DARWIN

July

The 27 Japanese bombers which raided Darwin were supported by 15 fighters. They rained bombs on the north coast Australian town, apparently annoyed at the failure of their attacks by sea. The battle of the Coral Sea badly upset their plans. Blazing oil storage tanks presented a difficult task for the fire fighters. Every Australian was determined that the further violation of the soil of his homeland would be repaid time and time again until the Japs scream for mercy. Only until then would they feel justice was done.

Across the Coral Sea is Port Moresby, a key base in New Guinea. Full shiploads of war supplies were unloaded in a hurry, for there was danger of Jap bombers there, too. With the cargo safely ashore, the alarm sounded, everyone rushed for shelter. A big enemy force appeared overhead and went into attack as the defending anti-aircraft guns went into action with all its might. A rain of bombs fell all round the unloaded ship but there was not a single hit. Through hell-like scenes such as this it was amazing that supplies got through.

Anti-aircraft guns defending Port Moresby.

COMBINED OPERATIONS
ALL FORCES RAID ON DIEPPE

August

Across the Great Divide between the English and French coastlines where the Channel broadens, Britain struck at the German-occupied port of Dieppe. The eyes of the RAF saw it on the day when combined operations delivered the biggest raid so far carried out on occupied Europe.

Assault craft under bombardment at Dieppe.

Aboard one of the destroyers, heading across the Channel, were the men who were about to come to grips with the enemy. In assault landing craft and invasion barges of many kinds, (including tank landing craft in operation for the first time), travelled the men who loomed out of the protective smoke screen to battle their way on to the beaches and quays of Dieppe. The Canadians, who formed the major portion of the force, Britain's own Special Service Troops and detachments of fighting French and American Rangers had gone into the attack. For many savage hours they fought through the hail of German fire. Casualties were piling-up on both sides as the Canadians and their brother warriors fought in the nine-hour battle of Dieppe.

Outside the Dieppe basin, the ALCs crept into the beach under cover of the ship's guns, while high overhead came the ceaseless drone of warplanes. And the Boston bomber boys sailed in and rained down with a great number of bombs. The German defences were being well and truly plastered.

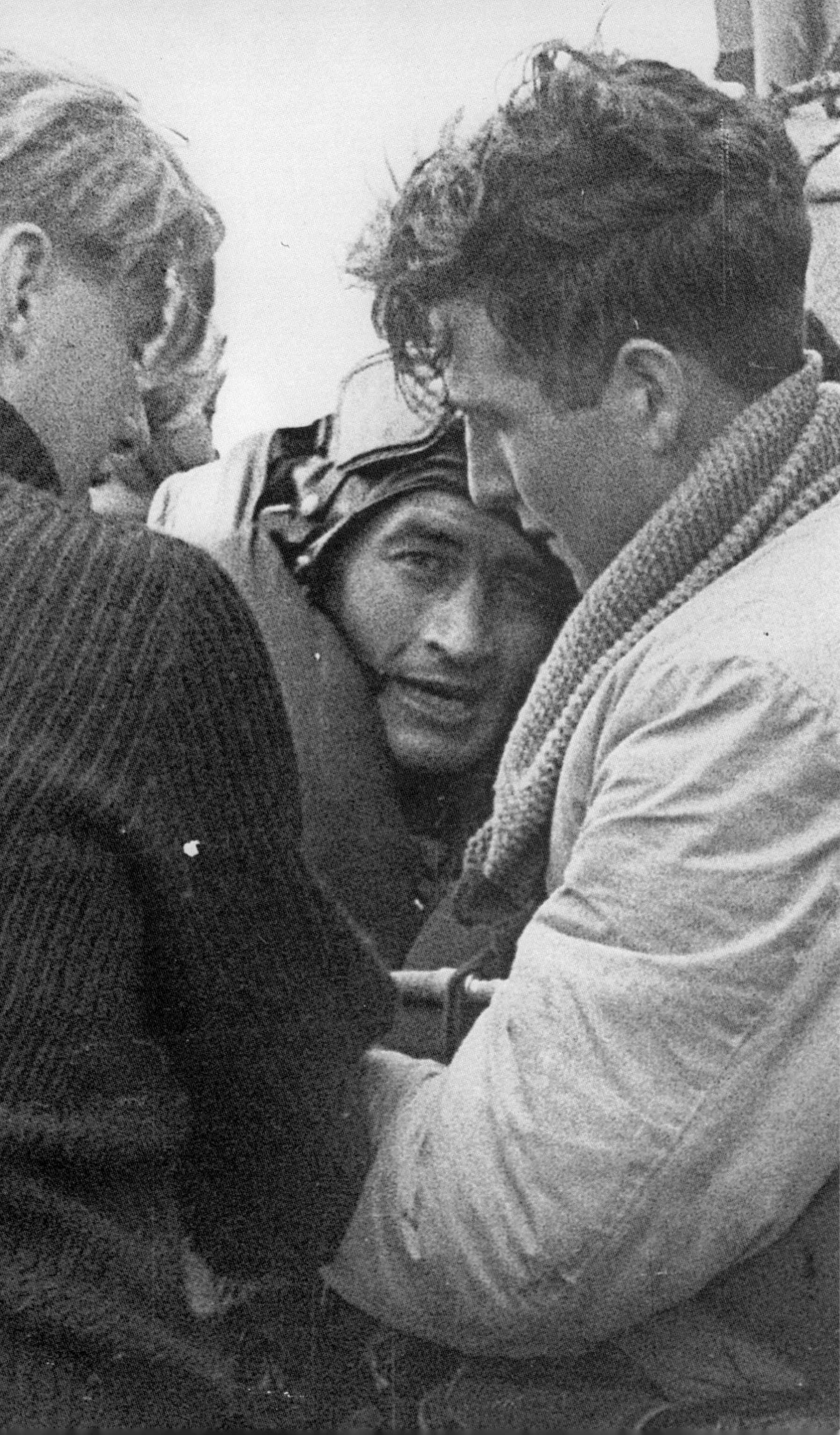

Six minutes after the time scheduled, re-embarkation began and with their task completed, the landing party started on their homeward journey. Behind them much of Dieppe was in flames; a pall of smoke drifted across the scene of stubborn fighting. All the way back, aerial combats were taking place. For hours the sky was filled with a milling host of fighters, as the biggest air battle ever fought saw aircraft falling from the sky like red autumn leaves.

A Spitfire circled the spot where a flight sergeant pilot baled out, and was seen floating on the supporting air sacks of his Mae West, a frequently-repeated incident but real life drama with a capital 'D'. Having kicked off his flying boots the pilot was hauled aboard with the help of many friendly hands and a good stout grab net. In spite of the ordeal he came up smiling. That boy deserved the applause.

Dieppe airman being rescued by destroyer.

The aftermath of battle always had its casualty lists. At ports along the south coast, Red Cross trains and ambulances waited to receive the wounded, men who had fought so heroically on the beaches, on the cliffs and in the streets of Dieppe.

Back to the green fields of England came the aircraft with men from the United Kingdom, Canada, New Zealand and our fighting European Allies at the controls. Those men had written yet another glorious page in RAF history. American airmen had also valiantly joined in the air battles which developed on a scale comparable to those fought during the Battle of Britain. The forces were aware that when they hit out again they would need no finer soldiers, ask for no better seamen than the sailors who for centuries ruled the seas and search for no nobler airmen. Europe awaited them.

Commandos return from Dieppe raid.

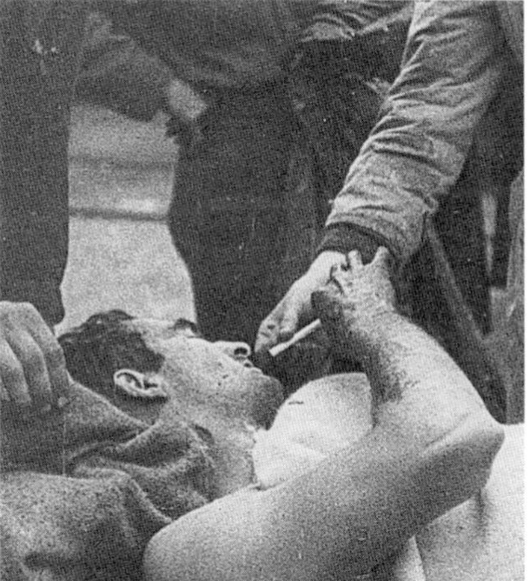

Return of wounded survivors of Dieppe raid.

Servicemen wounded in Dieppe raid arrive back in Britain.

MALTA RECEIVES ITS GEORGE CROSS

September

Malta's glorious resistance to the enemy was suitably honoured in the bomb-battered Palace Square, Valetta, when Lord Gort VC, Governor and Commander-in-Chief, presented the people of Malta with their George Cross.

Sir George Borg, the Chief Justice, received the decoration for the citizens. He then took the casket containing the Cross and the King's letter which accompanied it to the stand from which the people of Malta could view their cherished honour, until such time as it was taken to every village and town on the island. No people on earth had withstood as much as the loyal and stout-hearted Maltese who now read the King's words of admiration.

Lord Gort presents the George Cross, which then goes on display.

BATTLE OF THE SOLOMONS

November

Heavily-protected convoys ploughed through rough seas to bring American reinforcements for the fighting Marines on Guadalcanal. In the South Pacific war zone units from the three services make their surprise attack on the stategic base which the Japanese fought to recover.

U.S. marines storm ashore in the Solomons.

A fresh Marine force moved in to support the initial successful landing. Further evidence of aerial combats taking place in the vicinity showed a fighter going into the sea out of control. The determined Japanese effort to regain Guadalcanal was indicative of the importance they placed on the island. If they were to win it back, the threat to Australia would be all the stronger.

The struggle was concentrated round a vital aerodrome off Lunga. When the Marines walked in they found the airfield still burning as a result of heavy bombing. Large quantities of Japanese equipment were captured.

This was the rosy side of the fight, for the general situation had since deteriorated. Guadalcanal was still a hotly-contested base. Flame throwers were among the variety of weapons left behind. Deeply enraged by their initial reverse, the Japanese were out to stage a comeback. MacArthur's Marines were shouldering a big responsibility.

PREMIER IN THE MIDDLE EAST

August

A Lockheed Hudson touched down at a desert aerodrome bringing a mysterious passenger, Mr Bullfinch. No disguise, but a fine collection of hats and clothing for the secret visit to the Middle East. General Auchinleck met the Prime Minister at the start of his visit to the Egyptian war zone. Mr Churchill went straight up the line, making personal contact with South African fighting men, a very important part of his busy programme.

Churchill with gun crew and at lunch in the desert.

Travelling to El Alamein, the Prime Minister made a point of talking to a gun crew, men of a Royal Artillery Regiment doing stout work with a four point five. Mr Churchill's visit was a typical Winstonian surprise. The breezy friendliness went down well with the boys, not least of all with the Australians, one of whom, on discovering the sun-hatted visitor, exclaimed "Cripes it's old Winnie".

At a base landing ground the High Commissioner for Egypt, Sir Miles Lampson, Sir Alexander Cadogan and General Wavell awaited the Prime Minister's arrival in the giant Liberator 'Commando'. Mr Churchill was now wearing the uniform of Air Commodore. The Prime Minister as guest of honour was invited to lunch at the Officers' Mess.

Unfortunately, the Pathe cameras were able to record only the incidental progress of the Prime Minister's tour. Behind the scenes, far-reaching and important plans were being made and a start of far bigger things, embracing not only the Middle East but the Soviet Union and India. Mr Churchill's talks with King Farouk and President Stalin made this known.

After lunch he left the tent and made his way through an enthusiastic crowd. With General Smuts in Cairo, Churchill carried the baby again, the son of Sir Miles Lampson. With him was the great South African General Smuts, General Auchinleck (since succeeded by General Alexander), Generals Wavell and Brooke, Mr Casey, Admiral Harwood and Air Chief Marshal Tedder.

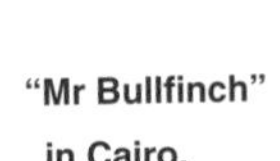

"Mr Bullfinch" in Cairo.

ROMMEL ON THE RUN

November

Britain was pleased to remember the 5th November, when the Eighth Army was making bonfires with the Axis troops in the desert, with the shattering effect of Rommel's full-scale retreat.

The wonderful news was let loose to the world and it was then that the first dramatic announcement telling of Britain's victorious advance was broadcast. By direct transmission from Cairo, Godfrey Talbot, the BBC war correspondent in the Middle East, radioed his electrifying despatch. Reproduced here are his historic words.

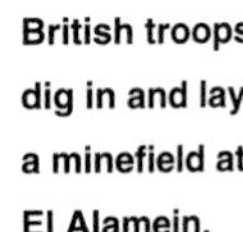

British troops dig in and lay a minefield at El Alamein.

"Out in the desert, out of Cairo there has come tonight the news for which we have been waiting. The news that all the world that fights for freedom has been waiting to hear, the news that the desert and Cairo have been expecting to be let loose all day. The Axis forces in the desert are in full retreat. There is no shadow of doubt about it, the enemy are on the run and we are after them. Right on their heels, no half measures. Maybe some of the enemy did get out, but there would be others in flight before the Eighth army, or dead. It is heartening news indeed tonight. Heartening to the United Nations and to the Eighth Army".

The order of the day was "Wipe out the Axis in Africa". Every communique told of how the German and the Italian columns were being relentlessly pursued and destroyed. Day and night there was no let-up in the hammering. The Montgomery 'mincing machine' was chewing the Afrika Korps to shreds.

Outstanding in the battle was the RAF maintaining a non-stop onslaught on the broken enemy streaming back. The greatest British success of the war overseas had been struck at Rommel, Germany's ablest commander was out-generalled and out-fought by the Allies.

A great toll of enemy prisioners was mounting daily. Nine thousand were taken in the first few days; then a further four thousand more were quickly added. In haste to save their own skins the Germans left three divisions of Italians to their fate. Present at the scene were the men whose names echoed round the world, General Alexander, Britain's C-in-C Middle East and General Montgomery, Commander of the Eighth Army who had won a glorious victory, thanks to the imperishable British soldier.

Preparing British fortifications at El Alamein.

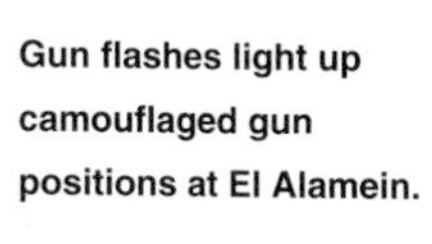

Gun flashes light up camouflaged gun positions at El Alamein.

Allied tanks moving up
at El Alamein.

Troops advance across El Alamein desert and capture a German tank crew.

OUR GREAT ADVANCE-MIDDLE EAST OFFENSIVE...continued

November

Pathe captured the latest pictures of the Nazis' November nightmare in the Middle East: a pictorial document illustrating the great advance through Egypt into Libya.

British troops advance in the Middle East.

The unrelenting pressure on the retreating enemy was kept up by land and air. With the Axis defences completely broken and the Afrika Korps on the run, the big chase began. With no time even to evacuate equipment, dozens of Nazi aircraft at Fuka aerodrome were left behind due to the rapid Eighth Army's advance. German gliders used for transporting troops were also hastily abandoned in the headlong flight west.

One of the biggest captures was General Ritter von Thoma, Commander of the Afrika Korps, who fell into the bag with many of other desert wild fowl. On arrival at the advance headquarters he was met by General Sir Bernard Montgomery - a generous victor.

Mersa Matruh harbour was now a graveyard of sunken supply ships and battered wharves; a wrecked seaplane occupied the foreground. One thing that stood out in this wonderful story of success was the overwhelming numbers of prisoners taken. If the men were too busy to bring them back, thousands trudged back without a guard, throwing their hats in and walking out of the war. Masses of heavy tanks were soon speeding out of the town for their next objective. Half a dozen dilapidated men came forward to surrender as British troops marched into Tobruk. Booby traps and landmines were plentiful and it paid to tread warily.

Once again in Tobruk there is the question of substituting flags. Across the face of the desert there moved a swarming mass of men. Without exception this was the most amazing sight yet seen. Thousands of half-starved Italians came streaming in. Isolated bodies joined up with the tattered tribe of lost men. Pathe's pictorial trek across Libya ended with one more tribute to General Montgomery. This was the hour of strong men such as he. "Westward look the sky is bright".

British take prisoners at Mersa Matrûh.

Captured General Ritter von Thoma shakes hands with Montgomery.

Victorious General Montgomery looks over El Alamein.

Allies recapture Tobruk.

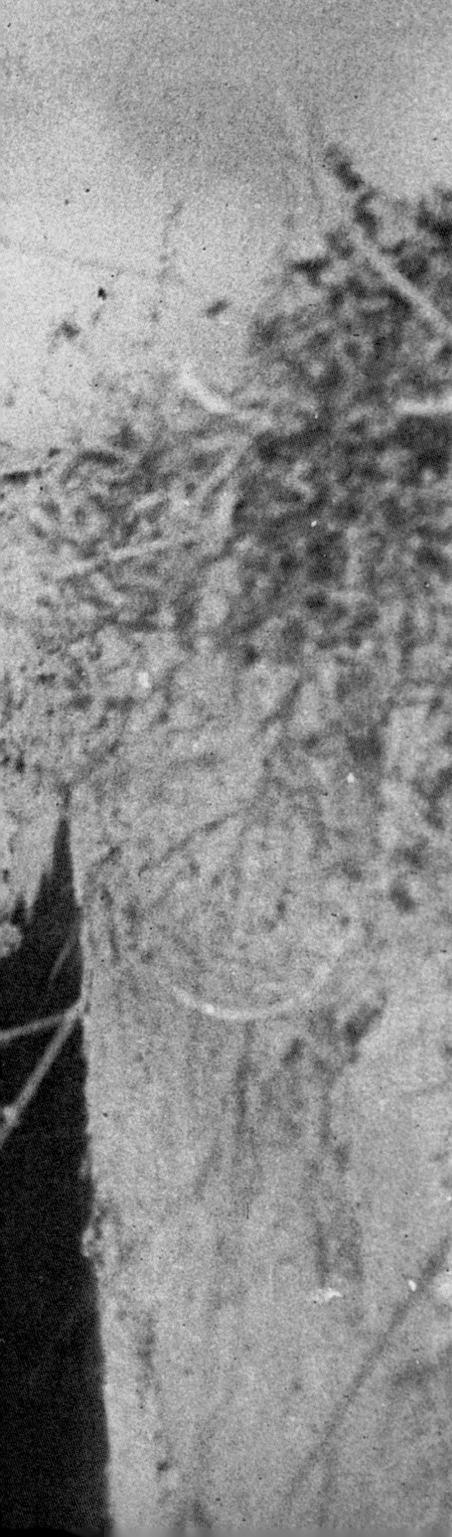

STALINGRAD THE UNCONQUERABLE

November

From the great steel city of Stalingrad, ghostly in its smoking heaps of shell and bomb-battered rubble, has emerged the most stupendous story of human courage and endurance. In this red hot hell, an appalling bombardment had reduced a noble city to wholesale ruin. Thousands died in the bloodiest siege of history. Day and night for months on end the defenders of Stalingrad fought the most glorious battle in Russian history.

On the city's outer perimeter, Red Army men maintained their stubborn resistance. Even though the once model city crumbled under the fire of German siege-guns they never gave in.

Many times the world expected the fall of Stalingrad but not so the defenders, who made every foot a death trap for the invaders. To win two buildings or fifty yards of roadway the Germans had to sacrifice hundreds of lives. Street fighting on an unprecedented scale decimated the Nazis, while the Soviet soldiers held on like grim death. Every square became a battle-ground, every building a fortress. The city of suffering refused to go down amid the gutted shells of buildings. In the reeking shambles of its streets, the ghostly remains of a population of half a million people completed a terrible existence. It did not look like a city capable of victory but by the most superb feat the city of Stalingrad triumphed.

Russian offensives in Stalingrad.

Battle of Stalingrad.

Sir William Beveridge talks about National Insurance and the Security Plan.

A nation at war

Britain had grown accustomed to the hardships of war. The blitz continued but soon other towns started to feel the power of the Luftwaffe. The RAF had started to bomb cities in the Baltic states, which so infuriated Hitler that he decided to retaliate by launching his so-called Baedeker raids. He ordered that every town mentioned in the Baedeker Guides to Britain should be obliterated. Exeter, Bath, York and Norwich were hit. Later in the year Canterbury also suffered from a German version of saturation bombing.

Britain also had troubles within the Empire. In India, Gandhi had continued his campaign of civil disobedience. Sir Stafford Cripps travelled to India to calm the situation and the country was promised Dominion status.

The thoughts of politicians and academics were not monopolised by the war. The famous Beveridge Report came out in 1942 which became a landmark in the social history of Britian. In the report, Sir William Beveridge, a leading Liberal, outlined proposals for the setting-up of a Welfare State. The Social and Health Services Britain enjoyed after the war were a direct result of that report.

Bomb damage in Canterbury.

During Indian civil disobedience riots.

BARCLAYS

PRINCESS ELIZABETH'S BIRTHDAY

April

Princess Elizabeth celebrated her sixteenth birthday by inspecting the troops as the new Colonel of the Grenadier Guards, at a special parade at Windsor Castle. The occasion also marked her entry into the official life of the nation. Her Royal Highness the Colonel walked to the long ranks of the Guardsmen followed by the King and Queen and Princess Margaret. Wearing the gold grenade badge of the Grenadiers in her hat, Princess Elizabeth made her first military inspection.

With the first part of the parade over, Her Royal Highness went to the dais where, with the King at her side, she took the salute as the Regiment marched past. This colourful ceremony in the castle quadrangle was one of the first functions to be held on that busy day when the Princess celebrated her 'coming out'. The final posed picture taken at the end of the review was regarded as a record of the first offical occasion in the life of England's future Queen.

Princess Elizabeth inspects the Grenadier Guards.

SIR STAFFORD CRIPPS IN INDIA

April

Their Excellencies the Viceroy and Marchioness of Linlithgow welcomed Sir Stafford Cripps on his arrival at New Delhi for consultations with leaders of Indian political parties. First to confer with him was Maulana Abul Azad, President of the Congress. Mr Jinnah, leader of the Muslim League, arrived in a cheerful mood.

Civil disobedience riots in India.

Sir Stafford's task had been described as the most delicate mission in the history of the British Empire. Representatives of the Princes are the Chancellor and Vice Chancellor of the Chamber of Princes. In white is the Chancellor, His Highness the Maharaja of Nawanagar, and with him is the warrior ruler, His Highness the Maharaja of Bikaner. Also present was Sir Henry Gidney, leader of the Anglo-Indians and Domiciled Europeans. The Sikhs sent delegates to represent their important community.

Pandit Nehru, one of the most important political figures in India, had one of several meetings with Sir Stafford while in company with Maulana Abul Azad.

The Mahatma Gandhi, clad in his loin cloth and shawl, entered strongly into the discussions which, although destined to reach a deadlock, would at least provide a basis for future negotiations.

Sir Strafford Cripps enjoys a joke with the Mahatma Gandhi.

INFORMATION
ASK ME

ROYAL VISIT TO BATH

May

The King and Queen went to see how Bath took its place in Hitler's plan of war. Once again the distorted German mind that conjured hopes of breaking British morale experienced the same indomitable spirit that prevailed during the days of the Battle of Britain. The bombed cities reflected this spirit.

From Buckingham Palace, mobile canteens were sent by Their Majesties to bring help and comfort to the homeless and civil defence workers. Destruction and death, were not new to Britons but, where once they suffered them and looked to the time when they would give back as much as they took, today the hour of retribution was with them.

Night after night, day after day, Britain was making the Nazis suffer with colossal air attacks. Where once they sent tens of aircraft, now it was hundreds, and to avenge the huge losses to their war machine, the Germans would turn the pages of a traveller's reference book to pick out Britain's beauty spots and historic landmarks for destruction. Bath was famous for both but her fame was now found in such people as the special constables who suffered severely, as did the fire fighters and wardens, rescue parties and nurses.

The people of Bath were famous and Their Majesties recognised this by walking among them with words of sympathy and praise. No threat of "historical reprisals" would cause diversion from the policy of heavy and still heavier bombing of Germany. While the Germans concentrated their bombers on targets suggested by Mr Baedeker, the RAF continued to open up the second front in the skies over Germany.

Civil defence warden talking to the Queen.

THE FLATTENED CITIES OF ENGLAND

During the Nazi bombings of 1940 and 1941, 2,500,000 private homes were damaged and 130,000 destroyed. Clean-up work continued during 1942, as damaged buildings were made safe or torn down entirely, protective fences erected, and some sites were totally levelled ready for re-building.

Much of the bombing "actually profited the nation by wiping out old, cramped, ill-lit, uneconomical buildings". Plans were already being drawn up to turn the empty spaces into green belts in garden cities.

HULL

In this cleared space behind Princes and Queens Docks, looking down Prospect Street (right), an air-raid warden has built his hut.

A chapel used to stand in the little triangle in the foreground. The usual wooden fences have been built around most of the cleared spaces, to save pedestrians in the blackout.

BRISTOL

Looking west in Bristol, over the wreckage of the 500 year-old St.Peter's Church at far left, past the cupola of All Saint's Church, to the hill tower erected to John Cabot, who sailed from Bristol.

Business as usual for the news theatre, showing a topical new navy serial, as well as Pathe News.

MR CHURCHILL'S TOUR

May

Wearing his uniform of Air Commodore of the RAF, Mr Churchill made an inspection of the bomber station during his round of visits in the North East. Among other places is a Tanks Corps training ground where the Prime Minister made his inspection while seated on the gun turret of a Covenantor.

The Prime Minister touring a munitions factory somewhere in the North East.

An inspiring sight came with a massed formation of tanks and aircraft driving and flying past the saluting base.

The Prime Minister's party, which included Dr Evatt, the Australian Minister of External Affairs, later made a tour of a munitions factory where Mr Churchill tried his hand at one of the machines. The operator was able to show him how she controlled her section of the production line. Later, Mr Churchill exchanged a kiss for a cigar given to him by one of the women factory workers.

From there he travelled to where 25,000 people had gathered outside Leeds Town Hall to hear words of encouragement on the work Britons were doing in the war effort. The Prime Minister laid emphasis on the arrangements for meeting the enemy, commending the assistance of hundreds of thousands of active and willing hands.

Mr Churchill takes salute while inspecting Tank Corps.

The Queen bowls a wood at Blantyre.

Cheering the King and Queen in Scotland.

KING & QUEEN IN SCOTLAND

June

To the accompaniment of much hearty cheering, a river steamer brought the King & Queen (during their comprehensive tour of Scotland), to one of the many industrial centres north of the border. Men of the Royal Navy, Merchant Service and the shipyard workers were among those to be specially honoured. At Paisley, Her Majesty was greatly interested in the work done at a day nursery for the children of war workers.

Edinburgh and Glasgow gave Their Majesties a great reception and at the latter city, firemen and women of the National Training Centre demonstrated their skill in the use of all types of appliances.

On to Blantyre, Lanarkshire where at the Miners' Welfare Centre the Queen was invited to test her aim on the bowling green. Her Majesty sent down a wood that would please many a professional. Those scenes and many others like them illustrate the warm welcome which Scotland extended to the Royal visitors.

Day nursery at Paisley.

HOLIDAYS AT HOME THIS YEAR

June

Spending holidays at home played an important role in the war effort and Pathe helped to advise Britons how they could best enjoy their holidays with this report.

First official fishing season in the Serpentine.

"It is vital that all transport is left free for the war effort so we really must spend our holidays at home. After all, the same sun shines on your garden or local swimming pool as on the beach at Tiddley-push-on-Sea.

There's an old saying that a change is as good as a rest, but it's just as true to say that a rest is as good as a change. You needn't go far for most of the holiday pastimes you've enjoyed in the past. Surely there's a river or lake fairly near to home; tennis courts are everywhere.

Dancing on the lawn is being arranged by many local authorities, while bands will play in most of the parks. It's a good opportunity to catch up on the films you've missed, while rod and line can bring big surprises. How much nicer

In Hyde Park.

your garden or allotment will be, after you and the family have spent extra time on it and how much nicer that little drop of er... ginger pop will taste.

If you like an energetic holiday,how about a spot of cycling or hiking in pleasant company? What a chance to improve your golf handicap on the nearest course or spend a lazy day watching cricket with an alfresco tea to follow. These few suggestions will surely show how you can spend a happy holiday at home instead of impeding the war effort by using transport needed for serious purposes".

Cultivating their hobby
in the allotment.

Londoners enjoying a cup of tea and a dance in the park.

At the open air pool.

MOBILE LAUNDRY

July

Yes, they were all a-blowin and a-blowin in the balmy breezes of a North country town. Mums, dads and grandpas were pleased to see that the mobile laundry had arrived and, instead of women having to go down to the river as they did in the past, they could now bring their clothes to the travelling laundry. Bundles of mischief and bundles of washing at the same time. So, as the boilers coped with all the washing, the housewives, if they liked, would go to the pictures. The touring wash house catered for every branch of the laundering art.

Grateful housewives bring their washing to mobile laundry.

Grandpa's "combies" blowing in the breeze.

THE KING WITH THE HOME GUARD

The King, who recently became Colonel-in-Chief of the Home Guard, paid a visit to units training and exercising in the South Eastern Command. One of the many Home Guardsmen with whom the King spoke to was Lance-Corporal Robey, son of a comedian. When asked if he was following in his father's footsteps he replied that he is on the staff of the Director of Public Prosecutions.

The King was shown a new submachine gun, the Sten, an automatic weapon now being issued to the Home Guard. Before leaving, the King made a point of saying how much he had been impressed by all he had seen.

The King chats to troops on a visit to a Home Guard training unit.

RECORD SALVAGE CAMPAIGN OPENS

August

Syd Walker was in search of old gramophone records in the nationwide British Legion Salvage Campaign.

He joined the campaign to add to the millions of worn and unwanted gramophone records needed for the recovery of shellac, an essential commodity in the manufacture of records.

The broken pieces were pulverised and the dust fed on to heated rollers which produced the plastic base for new discs. After passing through a variety of processes, the sheets of basic material emerged as new records under the giant presses which turned out the finished article. These were destined to play an important part in war. Factories, hospitals and the men in enemy prison camps would profit by the response to the appeal.

"That was a good one!" Syd Walker collects old records for salvage.

CALLING ALL STARS

September

Stars of the screen were called in to 'twinkle' for charity in a great Washington round-up. At a mass get-together, plans were made for the picture celebrities to go places and raise money and if you wanted an autograph it was all yours for the paying.

Secretary Morgenthau welcomed the visitors. When Hollywood came to Washington it was indeed a moving picture and what better missionaries for charity than the stars of the silver screen? If you wanted to see them in person the accent was on the purse. Greer Garson, otherwise Mrs Miniver, was busy at work raising money. Smallest contributions were thankfully received and written acknowledgments could be sold and proceeds handed to charity.
Hedy Lamarr accepted the applause while her fountain pen was kept very busy. Charm charity was a good choice; after all it was in a good cause.

Greer Garson surrounded by eager fans.

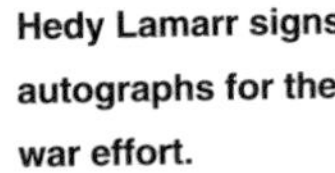

Hedy Lamarr signs autographs for the war effort.

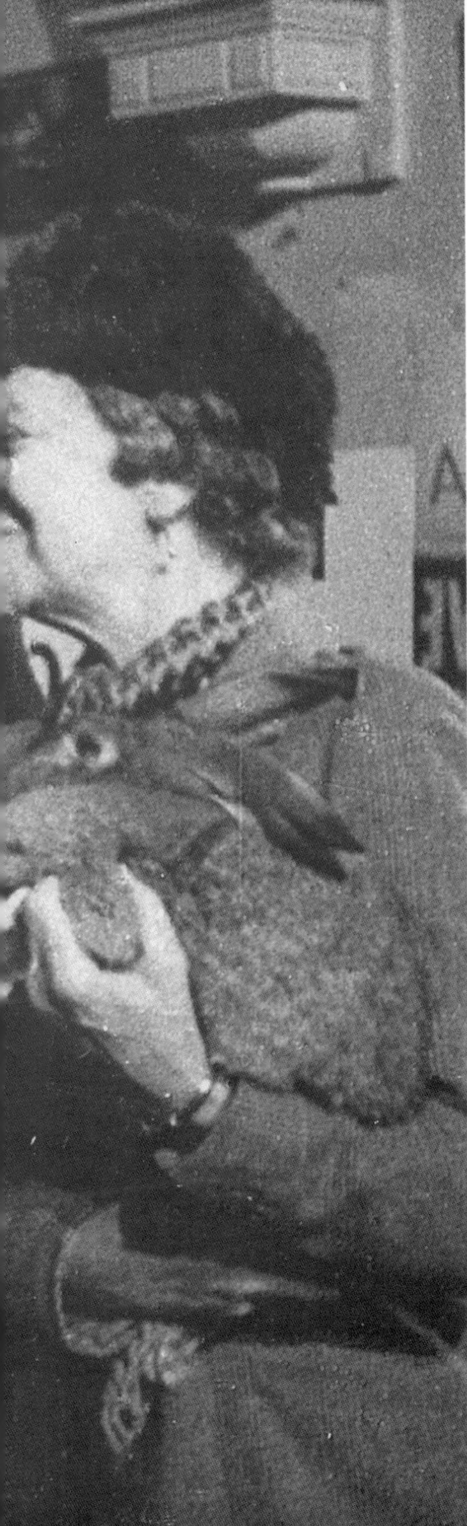

MRS ROOSEVELT VISITS LONDON

October

The whole of Britain rejoiced as out of the Royal coach stepped America's First Lady to be greeted by her host and hostess, the King and Queen. A great moment and one which lost all formality in the warmness of a friendly atmosphere. Representing the U.S. armed forces were General Eisenhower and Admiral Stark. The modest and endearing personality of Mrs Roosevelt made itself felt from the outset.

She set herself a full and comprehensive programme. One of her early visits was to St. Paul's Cathedral at the start of her tour of the City and the East End, with its many evidences of the Blitzkrieg days.

During her tours in company with the King and Queen, Mrs Roosevelt repeatedly referred to the spirit of "Mr and Mrs Everyman", which to that day still shone through the scarred face of London.

Then our friendly visitor went to Stepney, still pursuing her sympathetic enquiries and at all times avidly absorbing all she saw. A self-styled learner of British methods in many things, wherever she went she stored up a wealth of information to pass to the President. Women in uniform particularly interested her but just for the moment it was "John Citizen" of the East End who claimed her admiration.

Mrs Roosevelt visits Barham Village Bazaar.

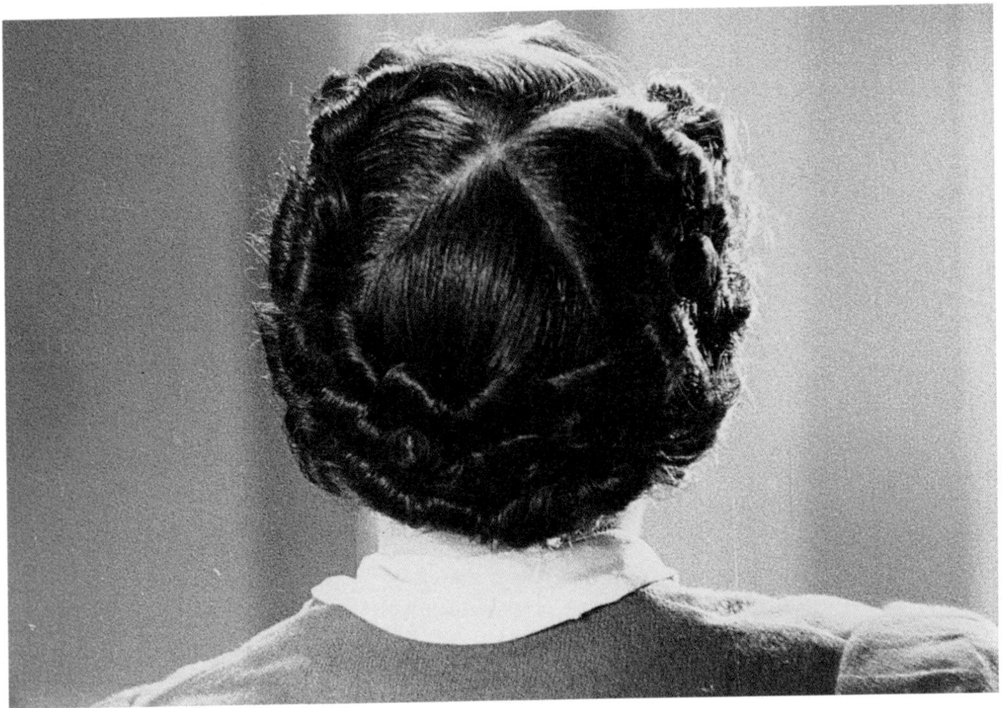

'Vingle' hairstyle.

THE 'VINGLE'

The 'Vingle' hairstyle was introduced as the short-cut for Victory. If your war job was where the wheels were turning, it was only common sense to play safe and keep your hair short. The special style incorporated partings forming four V's, hence 'V-ingle', and kept hair tidy and out of machines. Although women were giving their services to the war effort, there was no reason why they should give their complexion, too.

WOMEN AT WORK

July

More women were coming into industry everyday and their jobs were greatly varied. Women were tackling jobs which were thought impossible a few years previously.

Women had also advanced to driving cranes and they had justified themselves at similar tasks which required care and judgment. Then there was shipbuilding; women were taking to this job like ships take to water and girl riveters were fast becoming as skilful as the men.

Painting was another task carried out by women. It was apparent that they had risen to great heights with brush in hand and pot in reserve, as they busily painted a railway bridge to keep the crossing clean and bright. They had given that old bridge a new coat, so that they could buy a new one.

Women workers leave factory.

Preparing tanks (sealing doors etc.) before shipment to the Soviet Union.

Assembling Lancaster bomber.

WAAF mechanics checking bomber from North America.

WAAF in Ferry Command office.

Anti-aircraft emplacement.

WEIGHT AND SEA

August

When a group of large bathing beauties took to the pool for a swim, Pathe's cameras were there to get in on the action. This was their report.

"Now we know why tide rises and falls. When these cuties hit the drink, even in a New York swimming pool, it must affect the sea level for miles around. The launching of the S.S. "Fatso" - her tonnage is a war-time secret of course - but she's so buoyant she bounces right out again. And this cruiser-weight has a displacement that all but empties the bathing pool. So long slim, we'll be seeing you, I hope. Yes, the camera can do what a crane can't. Mind your sides please, here comes Blossom. Here now is a triple threat. Three depth charges on a submarine hunt. Look out below... there they blow. Stream-lined bathing beauties that are super-buxom and bountiful. They're a sensation, every time they bounce, the place rocks."

Watch out, all you spectators, you're going to get wet.

Most of them didn't stay around for the second jump!

WAAF FLIGHT MECHANICS

October

At a West of England aerodrome, a squad of WAAF flight mechanics in business-like dungarees worked on the engines of Avro Anson and Oxford aircraft. Smart young girls with a flair for engineering.

Out on the tarmac we saw one of the test pilots giving a few words of advice. But not all their work was on the ground. With parachute packs in the proper place they set off on a flight to study engine performance. Listening to the engine's heartbeats and watching the rev counter as the advanced trainer aircraft take off. At 1,000 feet the girls had their eyes glued to the instrument panel and noted the readings on their charts. Technical training spread over many months had turned these girls into first class mechanics.

WAAF checks engine watched by airmen.

WAAF prior to training flight.

GOVERNMENT OFFICIAL

November

"For three years we have been waging a defensive war. Now we are going over to the offensive on land, on sea and in the air.

Every man who can fight is needed for fighting and it is up to the women of Britain to take over the incumbent duties. All three of the womens' services are now open to volunteers. Whether you are married or single, or between the ages of seventeen-and-a-half and forty-five, there is a job waiting for you, a job that must be filled.

Whatever job you are doing now if it is not of the most vital necessity, you can be released. Women are needed in the ATS, in the WRENS or the WAAF. You are vital to the offensive."

Cinema trailer: "Learn to Cook", encouraging women to enlist.

LEARN TO
COOK
THE A.T.S.
W.A.A.F.
AND
W.R.N.S.
NEED
YOU

Wrens in Middle East
mess tent.

1942

Pathe and the People

Apart from the dominating issues of the World War, Pathe continued to recognise the importance of various aspects influencing the lifestyle of Britons and allies.

From politics to extraordinary events, a memorable year was captured and the moments of suffering and victory, hope and resilience formed the everlasting memories which are represented in the following pages.

London: Government to take over coal mines in Britain.

U.S.: Rationing of petrol. Customers checked for ration cards.

London: Opening of new Waterloo Bridge, built throughout the Blitz.

A tiny section of London, just a few streets, gives an appalling picture of vanished life and a new wasteland of masonry and rubble. This picture looks south towards St. Paul's (dome in left centre) and the Thames.

Moorgate underground still operates in left foreground. Beyond runs cleared Fore Street to four-pointed tower (centre) of 500-year-old St Giles Cripplegate where Milton and Frobisher were buried, Cromwell was married and the Romans built their town wall.

Shakespeare lived in the mid-distance. Milton Street, running across the picture, used to be infamous Grub Street.

At far right is the parade ground of the Honorable Artillery Company; and beyond are the burial grounds of Bunyan, Defoe, Watts, William Blake and John Wesley.

The Barbican Centre was eventually built over much of this area.

London: Pencil sharpeners taken from civil servants to conserve pencils.

Suburban garden.

London: "House-building will be boosted before war ends" Government.

London: Fuel rationing postponed by government after widespread opposition.

Road safety becomes an important issue, as every day at least four children are killed and 80 seriously injured on the roads of Great Britain.

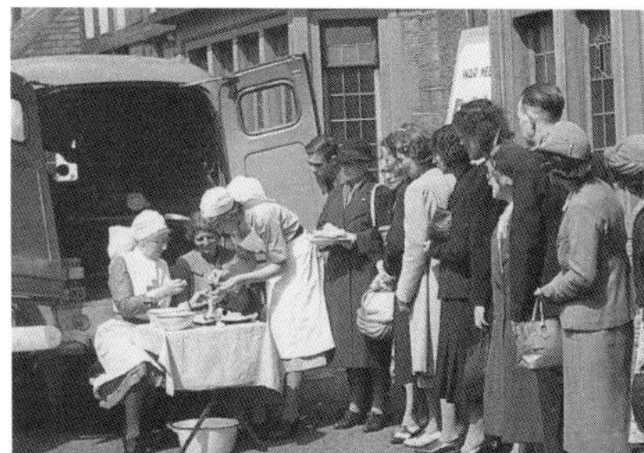

Blood donors queue in Tyneside town.

Washington: Wages, rents and farm prices frozen by President Roosevelt.

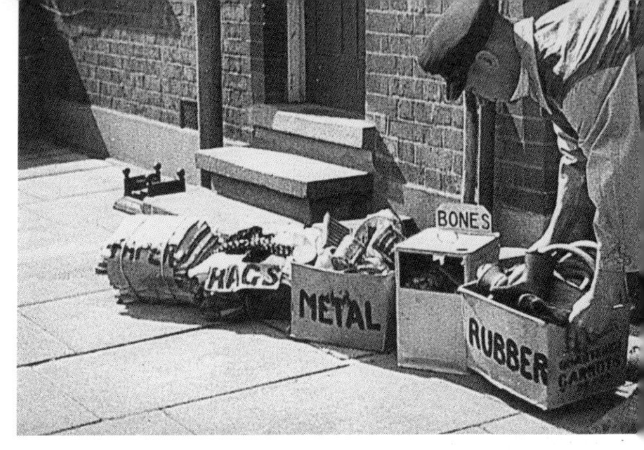

U.K.: Government bans pleasure driving.

London: Baking of white bread to be banned by government.

U.K.: Cut in milk ration to two and a half pints per week.

Confectioners are offering cardboard 'wedding cakes' for rent with icing made of chalk, as the real thing is no longer available. The Ministry of Food regulation says, "No person shall put sugar on the exterior of a cake after the same has been baked".

It was unlikely that shop-bought cakes would include more than 20 percent of oils or fats and no more than 30 percent sugar and to include no more than one covering of jam or chocolate.

Trailer: "Save salvage".

U.S.: Price freeze on major domestic items.

SAVE FUEL
on the
KITCHEN
FRONT

Trailer: "Save gas and electricity".

Playing cricket in school playground.

Child spectator in a crowd.

Women use cooked beetroot juice as lipstick.

US: Coffee rationing begins.

U.K.: Rose-hip syrup goes on sale nationwide; 2,000,000 more children get free cod liver oil.

In London, maximum clothes prices are laid down by the government; a suit must cost no more than £4 18s 8d.

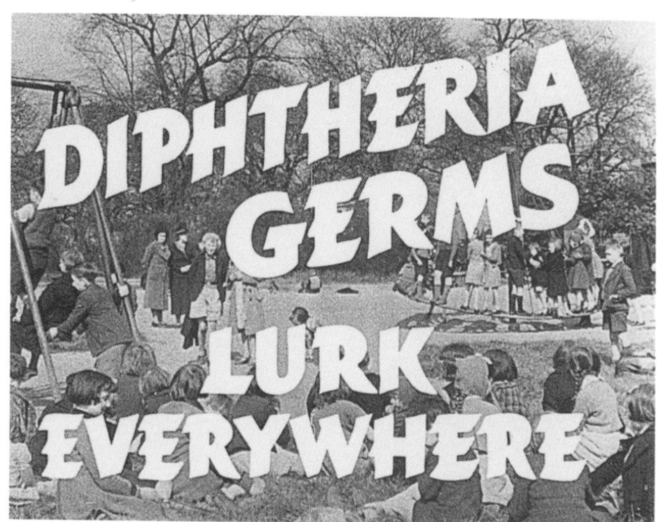

Diphtheria trailer.

U.K.: Sweet rationing begins.

Children at the fairground during factory workers' outing from Lancashire to Worsley.

All remaining Jewish schools in Germany are closed.

U.K.: Women need not wear hats in church, says Church of England.

Vatican allows women without stockings into St. Peter's, Rome.

London: Embroidery on women's underwear and nightwear banned.

U.K.: "Bare legs for patriotism" promoted for women's war fashions.

March 3rd

It's official; fashion trends are set to change and this time, instead of designers in Paris leading the way, styles will be dictated by the Board of Trade in London.

Fashion will become a strictly ;no-frills' affair, causing hemlines to rise as a direct result of the Board's new utility cloth combined with the limit on the number of styles.

Menswear will experience similar cutbacks, including no double-breasted coats, no sleeve buttons and no turn-ups on trousers. A standard price will be charged for utility suits made by tailors but the wealthier folk will still be able to buy the cloth and have it made up into 30-guinea suits by their Savile Row tailors.

American women enlisting, giving finger prints while signing up for war work.

The 'Vingle' hairstyle, with partings that formed four Vs, was introduced as the short cut for Victory.

London: Princess Elizabeth registers for war service, following her 16th birthday.

UNDERGROUND FACTORY

In a subterranean factory, British men and women are busy working and enjoying excellent environmental conditions - perfect ventilation, heating and lighting, combined with a full range of amenities.

At the Control Room, records of production are kept and bottle-necks in output prevented. Aircraft parts are being made at this particular factory, one of several in Britain and, despite its enormity, plans to extend it considerably are being undertaken.

Elsewhere, mammoth excavation work is under-way for yet another colossal underground factory and parts of it will be as much as 90 feet below ground.

Women and men constructing fuselage of Stirling bomber.

Waasies (Women's Auxiliary Service of South Africa) drove ambulances.

U.K.: Avro Lancaster heavy bomber, built in underground factories, is taken off the secret list.

Women prepare tanks (seal doors etc.) in preparation for shipment to the Soviet Union.

War worker checks guns of Defiant aircraft under construction.

King has 'Plimsoll lines' painted on Buckingham Palace baths to save hot water.

"A fighting man is sobbing. It is the boy whose letter never comes". Advertisement for Parker pens.

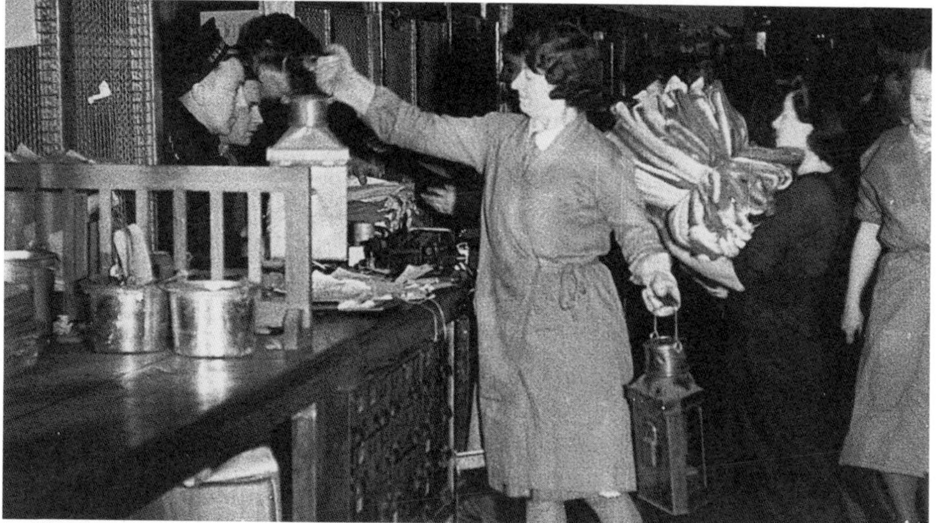

Supplying seamen at Naval Stores Depot.

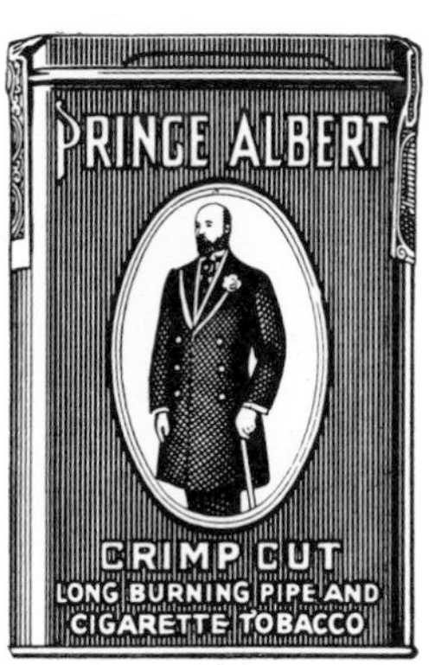

U.S.: Survey puts weekly food budget for family of five around $14.

Middle East mobile bath unit in Western desert.

213
25
213

SUPPLIES FOR OUR ARMIES

Tank and car engines costing up to a £1,000 each cover the floor of a store house at a Royal Ordnance depot. In an enormous spare-parts department, replacements parts of every conceivable kind are stored.

Hundreds of boxes of small-arms ammunition are piled in safe keeping deep underground, in miles of storage galleries and tunnels. An ammunition train with a load of shells arrives and soon a cargo of 4.5s is rolling along conveyor belts to the catacombs where thousands of tons of high explosives are put into storage.

The British Army is equipped with the finest guns in the world, among which is the 25-pounder gun-howitzer nicknamed the "Gunhow". Tanks for shipment to wherever fighting is thickest also came from this gigantic clearing-house.

A 'V' for Victory.

"Keep your eyes tuned to the victory pitch".

The White Ensign club provides shore-based entertainment for our sailors.

A friendly naval battle at the White Ensign club.

Ships and submarines are 50% scrap metal.

German battleships Scharnhorst and Gneisenau escape to Norway through English Channel.

LONDON WARSHIPS WEEK

At Trafalgar Square, London's Warships Week is launched with the aim of raising £125,000,000, sufficient to provide a fleet larger than that of the entire Nazi navy.

A large model of the superstructure of a battleship, complete with heavy and AA guns, dominates the square. On the second day of London's pageantry, detachments from all the armed forces and Civil Defence Services, almost 2,000 strong, formed a mile-long procession passing St. Paul's Cathedral and on through the City's historic highways. By black-out time on that first day, £28,000,000 had been raised.

7,700 aluminium pans make a persuit aircraft.

Parade through London during Warships week.

U-boats sank 900 Allied vessels in 1942.

Ticker tape welcome for war heroes in New York.

American troops marching to kit inspection in London.

Father Christmas brings presents to British children from U.S.

AMERICA CHEERS WAR HEROES

Amid a snowstorm of ticker-tape, fifteen selected war heroes, ten of them British, are greeted by crowds of wildly-excited and cheering New Yorkers on Broadway. The procession includes a cavalcade of courageous men from Vaagso, St Nazaire, Augsburg, Rostock and the Pacific, and passes on to City Hall for the official welcome.

Before an audience of 15,000 at Madison Square Garden, the climax of the great day is reached as the men who had won glory salute the British and American flags in a grand display of Anglo-American unity.

Later at the White House, Washington, President Roosevelt, together with Lord Halifax, receive the heroic men honoured for their courage and sacrifice, whose names were linked with the history-making attacks and battles which range from Lubeck to Pearl Harbour and to the Philippines.

American Expeditionary Force in Trafalgar Square.

'Pride of the Yankees'
Gary Cooper
Teresa Wright

'This Gun for Hire'
Alan Ladd
Veronica Lake

U.S.: Premiere of the ballet 'Rodeo' by Aaron Copland.

Best Films in 42 - U.K. Box Office

1. Mrs Miniver
2. The First of the Few
3. How Green Was My Valley
4. Reap the Wild Wind
5. Holiday Inn
6. Captains of the Clouds
7. Sergeant York

Moviegoers in their thousands are queueing to see Paramount's **'Holiday Inn'**, starring Bing Crosby and Fred Astaire side by side for the first time. The song-and -dance duo are a magic combination in the musical's easy-going format. Crosby's rendition of Berlin's 'White Christmas' is outstanding, delivered in his deceptively casual style. The success of the movie will be long remembered by a chain of motels named after it.

'Random Harvest'
Greer Garson
Ronald Colman

Other top Box Office films
Bambi
The Fleet's In
One of Our Aircraft is Missing

Douglas Fairbank Jnr during the King's visit to a U.S. warship.

Bing Crosby, Marjorie Reynolds, Fred Astaire and Virginia Dale in a scene from 'Holiday Inn'.

HAPPY
NEW
YEAR

Academy Awards
26th February

Best Picture
'How Green Was My Valley'

Best Director
John Ford
'How Green Was My Valley'

Best Actor
Gary Cooper
'Sergeant York'

Best Actress
Joan Fontaine
'Suspicion'

Best Sup. Actor
Donald Crisp
'How Green Was My Valley'

Best Sup. Actress
Mary Astor
'The Great Lie'

'Reap the Wild Wind'
Ray Milland, Paulette Goddard and John Wayne.

'Casablanca'
Ingrid Bergman
Humphrey Bogart.

Marlene Dietrich, owner of the loveliest pair of legs in Hollywood, insured them with Lloyd's of London for £1 million.

John Loder, Evan Evans, Donald Crisp, Sara Allgood, Richard Fraser, James Monks, Roddy McDowell, Maureen O'Hara, Patric Knowles in 'How Green Was My Valley'.

Gene Kelly, Judy Garland and George Murphy in 'For Me and My Gal'.

At the age of 30, Gene Kelly makes his screen debut in M-G-M's **'For Me and My Gal'**. He plays egotistical dancer Harry Palmer, who teams up with George Murphy and Judy Garland.

Kelly and Garland singing **'Oh, You Beautiful Doll'** and Garland singing **'After You've Gone'** and **'When Johnny Comes Marching Home'** were outstanding among the film's musical numbers.

'Mrs. Miniver' tops U.K. and U.S. box office ratings with a fantasy view of English village life.

'Playmates' in 1941 was John Barrymore's last film and during the three years before his death, he kept himself afloat on a sea of booze by parodying his own drunken decline. At the age of 60 he died a poverty-stricken man, of complications arising from a chronic liver and kidney ailment.

His funeral was attended by a crowd of celebrities and, among them, his old drinking and shooting companion Clark Gable made his first public appearance since the death of his wife Carole Lombard in January.

Clark Gable became a private in the U.S. Army having finished 'Somewhere I'll Find You' with Lana Turner.

Wartime regulations hit Hollywood now that America had entered the conflict. Within 48 hours of the attack on Pearl Harbour in December 1941, Army officials moved into all the studios, taking the firearms used in production and handing them to civil defence units. Night filming is temporarily halted and the studios have been put on a daylight shift of 8am to 5pm to enable employees to beat the blackout on the way home.

'Joseph and the Angel', Epstein's new scupture exhibited in London.

Director Ernst Lubitsch's new film, **'To Be or Not to Be'** has stirred critical controversy with some critics accusing the biting comedy of tastelessness. The film is based on the Gestapo and their war manoeuvres and stars Jack Benny and Carole Lombard. Unfortunately, the film's release had been overshadowed by the distressing news of Carole Lombard's death. While on a war bonds tour, the aircraft she was in crashed in mountains west of Las Vegas on 16th January 1942. Hollywood had lost an irreplaceable talent and her husband, Clark Gable, was devastated by the news.

Gert and Daisy help to form Street Saving Groups.

Vera Lynn, known as 'The Forces Sweetheart', with 'We'll Meet Again'.

Hits of 42

This is The Army, Mr Jones

White Christmas

We'll Meet Again

Bombed theatre in Bristol. Note the ironical label, 'SAFETY CURTAIN'.

SAFETY

17th January
U.S. boxer Muhammad Ali, born Cassius Clay (Louisville, Kentucky)

25th March
U.S. singer Aretha Franklin (Memphis, Tenessee)

27th March
Michael York (Fulmer, Buckinghamshire)

23rd April
Sandra Dee (Batonne, New Jersey)

24th April
Barbra Streisand (New York)

2nd June
Stacy Keach (Savannah, Georgia)

1st July
Genevieve Bujold (Montreal)

9th July
Richard Roundtree (New Rochelle, New York)

2nd November
Stephanie Powers
(Hollywood)

29th September
Britt Ekland
(Stockholm)

15th November
Daniel Barenboim
(Buenos Aires, Argentina)

Harrison Ford, whose films include American Graffiti, Star Wars, Force 10 from Navarone, Frisco Kid, Raiders of the Lost Ark, and Indiana Jones and the Temple of Doom.

Bob Hoskins, whose films include Royal Flash, Zulu Dawn, The Honorary Consul, The Cotton Club, Mona Lisa, and Who Framed Roger Rabbit?

17th November
Martin Scorsese
(New York)

26th October
Bob Hoskins
(Bury St Edmunds, Suffolk)

20th October
May Robson
(Beverly Hills, California)

16th January
Carole Lombard
(Nevada - Found dead in the wreckage of a TWA airliner)

Carole Lombard, who appeared in No Man of Her Own, Bolero, Twentieth Century, My Man Godfrey, Nothing Sacred, Mr and Mrs Smith, and To Be or Not To Be.

5th November
George M Cohan
(New York - Intestinal ailments)

7th May
Felix Weingartner

29th May
John Barrymore
(Hollywood - liver and kidney failure)

4th August
James Cruze
(Hollywood - Heart ailment)

25th August
Duke of Kent
(Aircraft Crash)

30th November
Buck Jones
(Boston, Massachusetts - Fire accident)

5th January
George Brent to
Ann Sheridan

10th January
Mickey Rooney to
Ava Gardner

12th January
Betty Field to
Elmer Rice

16th May
Laraine Day to
James Ray Hendricks

19th June
Marilyn Monroe to
Jim Dougherty

Marilyn Monroe.

17th July
Lana Turner to
Stephen Crane

2nd August
Ruth Hussey to
C. Robert Longenecker

23rd August
Fay Wray to
Robert Riskin

October
Gregory Peck to
Greta Konen

Cary Grant with his second wife, Barbara Hutton.

8th July
Cary Grant to
Barbara Hutton

26th January
Milburn Henke - first American soldier to set foot on British soil (Northern Ireland.)

1st January
Germany estimates that 131,823 Jews are still living in the country.

Politics and War

In 1942 the tides of war began to turn against the the Axis. In January, the Japanese occupied much of the Pacific and the Nazis were advancing in North Africa, the Eastern Front, and the Atlantic. But the Allies started to re-gain ground. Montgomery re-captured El Alamein in a decisive victory; the USSR smashed through the armies attacking Stalingrad; and the US forced the Japanese to withdraw from Midway Island and the Solomons.

Alliances were agreed between the Allied governments, while new faces were seen in the goverment at home. Britain's plans for full Indian independance after the war provoked a campaign of civil disobedience, after Ghandi's Congress party demanded immediate self-government.

19th January
General Sikorski and Stalin sign friendship declaration.

15th January
In India, Pandit Nehru is named by Gandhi as his successor.

4th February
Lord Beaverbrook appointed Minister of War Production.

9th February
American
Volunteer Pilots
defend Rangoon.

J. Edgar Hoover.

24th January
Prisoners along road after fall of Bardia, Libya, to British.

1st March
British paratroops raid and destroy a German radio-location station at Bruneval near Le Havre, returning with prisoners.

4th March
Sir William Jowitt is named post-war head of planning for reconstruction.

12th March
Lines of German prisoners captured on Russian Front.

1st April
The number of Jews in Germany falls to 51,257.

9th March
Bomber crews board Stirlings to bomb Renault works at Billancourt, Paris

26th March
The Nazis begin to deport Jews to Auschwitz concentration camp in Poland.

30th April
Hitler meets Mussolini in Salzburg.

7th May
The naval base of Diego Suarez, Madagascar, surrenders to the British forces.

11th June
Commandos return from raid on the Boulougne/Le Touquet area.

28th June
All Jews in occupied France over the age of six, must wear the Star of David.

6th July
Winston Churchill meets President Roosevelt in the USA for strategy talks.

10th July
After joining his troops for an expected triumphal entry into Cairo, Mussolini returns to Rome.

14th July
700 people in Yugoslavia slaughtered by Germans in reprisal for the killing of the Zagreb Gestapo chief.

1st August
Railway line from Stalingrad to Krasnodar cut by Germans.

6th August
Germans advance from the south towards Stalingrad.

31st August
Churchill greeted by his wife on his return from Moscow.

Close-up shot of Air Marshall 'Bomber' Harris C in C Bomber Command.

1st September
Shigenori Togo, Japanese foreign minister, resigns "for personal reasons".

Lancaster Bomber rolled out of hanger to start tests.

10th September
The RAF drops 100,000 bombs in under an hour on Dusseldorf.

13th September
100th raid on Bremen by RAF.

20th September
116 people in Paris murdered in retaliation for increasing attacks on German officers.

Lancaster
Bombers being
assembled.

23rd September
Allies advances force
Japanese to pull back
in New Guinea.

A Lancaster
Bomber
in flight over
countryside.

31st August
Malta convoy.
Gun crews in
action.

31st August
Cargo ship burns
in the distance
after attack on
convoy.

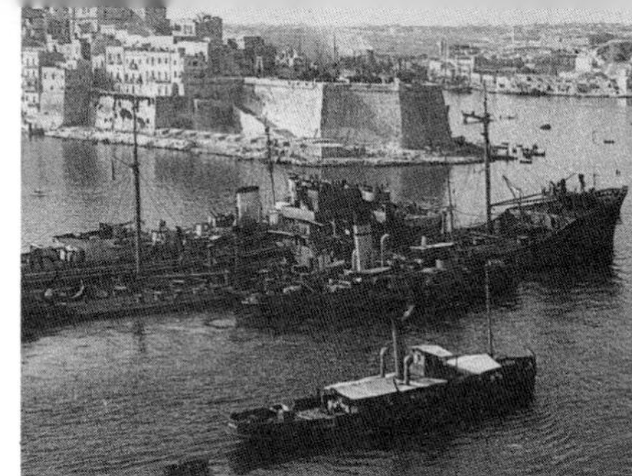

31st August
Damaged cargo vessels including Tanker 'Ohio' arrive in Malta Harbour.

28th September
Captain Mason of the tanker 'Ohio' awarded the George Cross at Palace Investiture.

21st September
Italian soldiers captured during the Malta convoy attack, led blindfold on board ship at Mediterranean port.

Mine sweeping in the Far East.

Desert Patrol comes under fire.

**17th September
Premier and
Home Guard.**

**17th September
Home Guard
give three
cheers to
Churchill at
Horseguard's
Parade.**

24th September
Food Minister Lord Woolton visits RAF canteen.

27th September
Offensive against the Japanese begun by General MacArthur's Australian and US forces.

6th October
16 year-old London galley boy, John Conroy wins the British Empire Medal for bravery on Russian convoys.

24th October
General Eisenhower leaves for North Africa, heading a giant task force.

30th October
Battle of El Alamein begins.

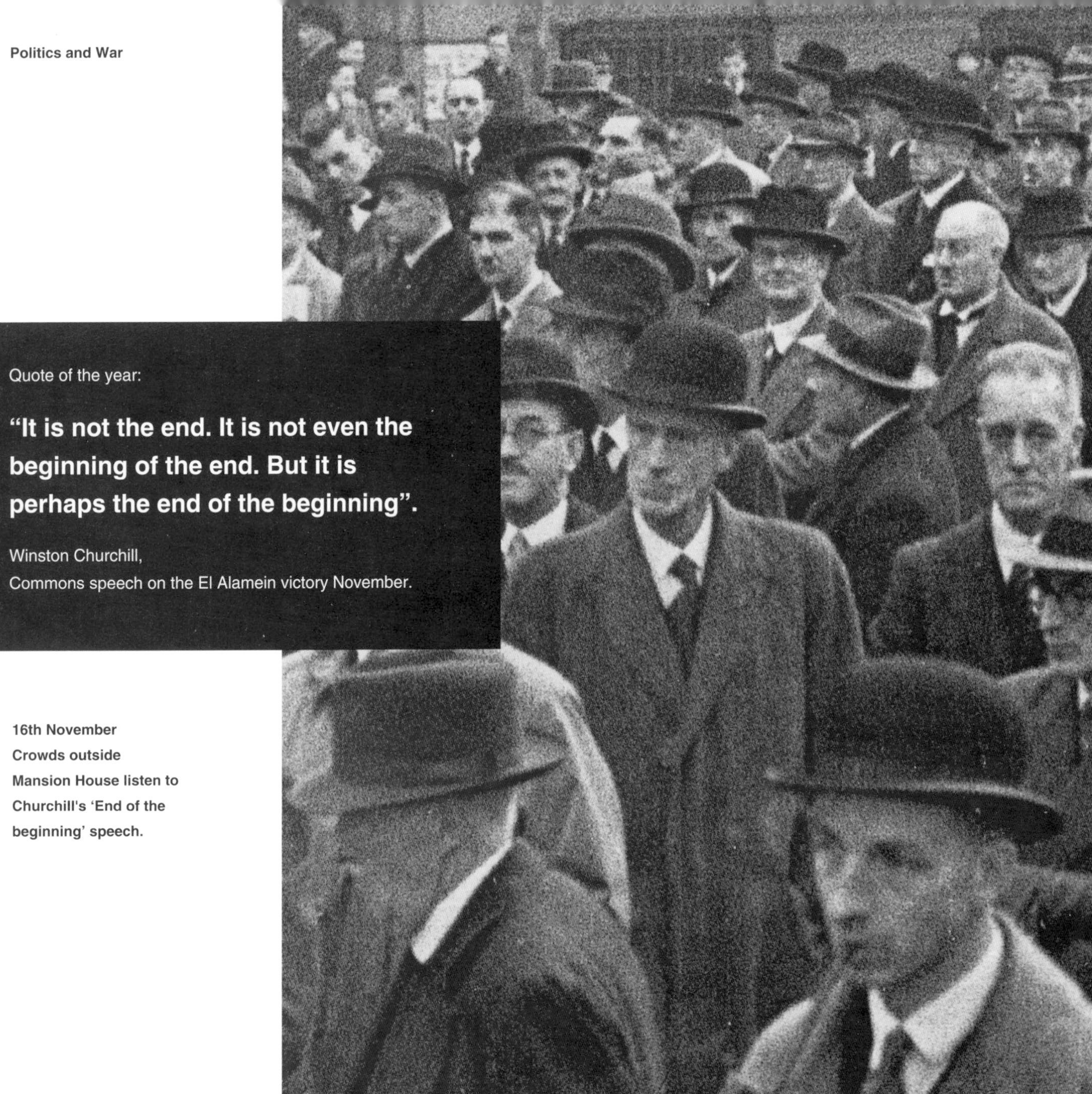

Quote of the year:

"It is not the end. It is not even the beginning of the end. But it is perhaps the end of the beginning".

Winston Churchill,
Commons speech on the El Alamein victory November.

16th November
Crowds outside Mansion House listen to Churchill's 'End of the beginning' speech.

22nd November
Herbert Morrison replaces Sir Stafford Cripps in the war cabinet.

26th November
Russian troops break through German lines at Stalingrad.

13th December
British Jews hold a day of mourning for the victims of Nazi genocide.

20th December
The Soviet Army attacks German forces on the Don.

30th December
12 prominent Vichy officials arrested by Giraud to prevent further assassinations.

France: Ex-premiers Blum, Reynaud and Daladier face a second trial for "causing the defeat of France".

Belfast: Police clash with IRA sympathisers after a 19-year-old Republican is executed.

London: The Allies take the first steps towards setting up a commission to investigate war crimes.

IRA shoot dead two policemen.

France: Ex-premier Edouard Herriot is arrested.

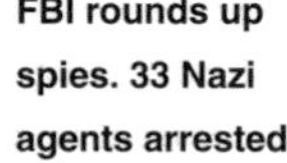

FBI rounds up spies. 33 Nazi agents arrested.

ENGLAND v. SCOTLAND AT WEMBLEY

The International "Aid for Russia" Match was held at Wembley Stadium, attracting 66,000 soccer fans to watch England versus Scotland.

Mrs Churchill went on to the field to shake hands with the English players and announced that the Prime Minister was back in England. King Peter of Yugoslavia and members of the Soviet Mission were also there.

It was Scotland's misfortune that England were playing the soundest set of defenders which had represented the country for many seasons. Three-nil in England's favour was the outcome and the gate money collected was donated to "Aid to Russia".

Enthusiastic supporters at the "Aid for Russia" football match.

U.S.: Heavyweight champion boxer Joe Louis tells pressmen "My fighting days are over".

U.S.: Washington Redskins beat Chicago Bears 14-6 in the National Football League championships.

MILLS/ HARVEY KNOCKOUT

The sensational Harvey-Mills fight attracted 30,000 spectators to Tottenham football ground for the World, Empire and British light-heavyweight championships.

Gordon Richards was again acclaimed champion jockey. He won this title 26 times.

Freddie Mills beats Len Harvey at White Hart Lane.

Pilot Officer Len Harvey lost the fight to defend his titles after his challenger Sergeant Freddie Mills finished the match with the "Mills Bomb", followed by a fusillade of lefts and rights.

Hopes of a Royal Derby win were shattered on Newmarket Heath when the third war-time Derby was won by "Watling Street" at 6-1. The King's horse "Big Game" was in sixth after starting a red-hot favourite.

BASEBALL IN LONDON

At Wembley, Mrs. Churchill greets members of the American and Canadian Forces who meet in a baseball match, before almost 10,000 spectators, in aid of the British Red Cross and St. John Fund....

Crowd at the match.

Baseball is rather like an intensive form of Rounders, with added pep and fireworks. It's certainly not a game which can be learned from a correspondence course. In the United States, baseball stars receive salaries comparable with Cabinet Ministers, front rank film stars, and (hm) newsreel commentators.

Trying to condense all the thrills of a baseball game within the limits of a newsreel is like trying to get a quart into a thimble - it just can't be done.

Canada beat the United States, and the Red Cross won the gate money.

U.S.A. verses Canada at Wembley.

Pathe's continual reports brought the year's major world events to its viewers and in its distinctive style also provided further pictorial news on a large variety of events ranging from lifestyle in Britain to amusing and interesting facts.

As the memorable year of 1942 ended, another began. On New Year's Day the USSR captured Velikiye Luki, splitting the German armies threatening Leningrad and Moscow, and leading to the eventual surrender of the remnants of the German Sixth Army. This set the pattern for the rest of 1943.

Although they still dominated the major theatres of war, the Axis were forced into a defensive role by the Allied forces. Montgomery's pincer attack from Egypt and Tunisia turned Rommel's retreat into a disaster for the Axis, all their North African forces surrendering in May.

The way was clear to invade Italy, and Mussolini resigned after Sicily was captured in July. By September the mainland of Italy had been invaded, peace with the Allies agreed, and war on Germany declared by Italy.

1943 saw Hitler's decisive defeat at sea and in the air. The Allies' strategic bombing raids on Germany, including the Dambusters' attack in May, caused havoc to German industrial and Military production. Improved Allied defences forced the Germans to withdraw their U-boats from the North Atlantic in May. Their subsequent return in September made little impact to the Allies' shipping. Germany's naval hopes suffered a grievous blow in May, when the *Tirpitz* was crippled, and again in December when the *Sharnhorst* was sunk.

In the Far East, the Japanese were also forced onto the defensive by the British forces in Burma, and the United States steadily recaptured the Pacific islands.

At the Teheran Conference in December, the Allied victories enabled their leaders to agree that the invasion of Western Europe should begin in the early summer of 1944.

ACKNOWLEDGEMENT

The idea to produce the **Year to Remember** books was born out of the successful **Year to Remember** videos which cover the years 1930-1969.

The British Pathe News library contains some 50 million feet of film dating back to the 1890s. And as such there are probably over 200 million stills of history which could be taken from the film.

Playing stills photographer with movie film is a wonderful task. My thanks go to Ron Saunders of British Pathe News whose knowledge of the library and events is unsurpassable. Special thanks also to the staff of Dennis Fairey and Associates who designed the book. Special mention to Jane Feiven, Jackie Thorn, Sylvia Leigh and Andrew Yeomans for their time, effort and enthusiasm.

Ninety percent of the photographs are taken from the Pathe Film Library and were printed by the Pinewood Stills Department. Inevitably some events which needed to be included were not covered by Pathe - so the following acknowledgements are:

Topham Picture Library
p.121, p.122, p.123, p.124, p.126, p.128, p.129, p.133.

The Hulton Picture Collection
p.130, p.132.